Keeping It Up!

Also by Cathy Hopkins and Gray Jolliffe

Girl Chasing: How to improve your game
Man Hunting: A girl's guide to the game
69 Things to Do When You're Not Doing *It*:
The in-between lovers handbook

Keeping It Up!

HOW TO MAKE YOUR LOVE AFFAIR LAST FOR EVER

CATHY HOPKINS
Illustrated by Gray Jolliffe

Fontana
An Imprint of HarperCollins*Publishers*

Fontana
An Imprint of HarperCollins*Publishers*,
77–85 Fulham Palace Road,
Hammersmith, London W6 8JB

A Fontana Original 1992
3 5 7 9 8 6 4 2

A catalogue record for this book is
available from the British Library

ISBN 0 00 637855 2

Set in Linotron 202 Sabon and Futura by
Rowland Phototypesetting Ltd, Bury St Edmunds, Suffolk

Printed in Great Britain by
HarperCollinsManufacturing Glasgow

CONTENTS

Introduction 9

1   **Love is** 11
2   **Moving in together** 15
3   **Passionkillers** 21
4   **Rescuing the romance** 30
5   **Sex** 36
6   **The secret** 42
7   **What the experts say** 52
8   **What the realists say** 57
9   **Infidelity** 64
10 **And finally** 67

'If you can keep your mate when all about you
are losing theirs and blaming it on you . . .'
                                    (Rudyard Kipling . . . ish)

INTRODUCTION

What fresh Hell is this?

'What fresh hell is this?'
Dorothy Parker

The first time my friend Derick used that particular quote, it
made his girlfriend laugh. He'd just met her family. After
he'd moved in with her, he started using it a lot.

He said it when:
he saw her first thing in the morning
he met her best and oldest friends
he found her knickers in the bathroom sink
her mother took over the wedding plans

So she started saying it when:
he got drunk, loud and obnoxious
he farted under the duvet
he stayed out late
he stopped talking to her.

What had begun as an endearing joke between them started
(amongst other things) to irritate them both. Now they've
split up. She's looking for a replacement who doesn't suffer
from wind. He's taken up flying and dating nineteen-year-
olds.

This book is about how to have a successful relationship
and how to avoid the hell whether fresh, frozen or served
with raspberries.

1

LOVE IS

> '*Before you love, learn to run through snow leaving no footprints.*'
> (Turkish proverb)

Impossible. Obviously some love-lorn poet trying to warn future generations that love and all that goes with it is not easy, not a rose garden, nor a bowl of cherries. So what the hell is it? Any other condition that causes such dramatic and strange changes in behaviour would by now have been thoroughly researched and a cure found (or at least a tablet one could take when the symptoms came on).

But no one took any notice of the Turkish poet then, and they don't now. Love makes the world go round we all smile, as couples bill and coo. 'Round the bend,' it should read. At least that makes more sense.

We all know the 'love is' cartoons: 'her smile in the soft light of the morning,' 'flowers when she's feeling ill,' etc. More like she's the Medusa in the morning. And if she's ill, he'll immediately develop something potentially terminal so as not to be outdone in the 'getting attention' stakes. I reckon Plato, who incidentally was the first to start the 'love is' series, had it right when he said, 'Love is . . . a grave mental disease.'

Love is:

Love is slowing the car right down to let her out

Running through the snow leaving no footprints is easy compared to having a 'relationship' with someone who claims to be of the same species but is *obviously* an alien. So why do we do it? Basically because everybody else is doing it, and you're thought 'a bit odd' if you don't too. It's said that love is blind so it's a clear case of the blind leading the blind.

One man said he fell in love and moved in with his partner because 'she gave me my first long look at a naked woman with the lights on'. Other people do it for more predictable reasons:

fear of loneliness
to have children
to have regular sex
to have a committed relationship
for security

> A skinny old maid named Dunn,
> Wed a short-peckered son of a gun,
> She said, 'I don't care,
> If there isn't much there,
> God knows it's better than none.'

out of desperation
because they're demented

According to recently conducted surveys serious relationships are making a comeback, but whether you've only just got involved, or are seriously committed or married, the learning curve in the beginning is the same. Sooner or later you have to know the truth about each other. She has to discover he's the bass player in a heavy metal band who practises Wednesdays and Fridays in the front room of his flat. And he has to meet her eight cats, three fish and her rabbit, Harvey, not to mention Veronica De Voile, her best friend and leader of the local Croatian-lesbian-single-mother's-socialist group who meet Wednesdays and Fridays in the front room of *her* flat.

But it's love. You vow to rise above it all, and move in together.

2

MOVING IN TOGETHER

> '*Any man who buys wallpaper, drapes or even a prayer rug on his own is auditioning for the Bureau of Missing Persons.*'
> Bill Crosby

It's a great theory that moving in with your lover is fun. You look forward to the day the truck arrives with all his/her worldly goods:

She: 'You *can't* be serious? You're not putting *that* up in *my* bedroom?'
He: 'Oh, it's *your* bedroom now, is it? Didn't take long, did it? What happened to *our*?'
She: 'OK, sorry, sorry. Of course, put it up. I've always secretly wanted a glow-in-the-dark dart board in *the* bedroom. Look, I thought this paper would look fabulous in the lounge . . .'
He: 'Yerrk! Hideous, you put that up and I'm off . . .'
She: 'But you only just got here!'

Early days can be one long fight. He likes the stark black-and-white, Japanese Zen look, she favours the comfy clutter of fading antiques. He's a night person, she's an early morning person. Her friends are valued, close and

supportive, she loves a house full of people, conversation and laughter. He only sees mates for playing squash and wants peace, privacy and quiet when he's at home. He likes documentaries on the Polish economy, the more subtitles the better. She prefers 'Blind Date' and 'Baywatch'.

The term 'opposite sex' goes for everything from the decor to the diet.

> 'Marriage is an alliance entered into by a man who can't sleep with the window shut, and a woman who can't sleep with the window open.'
>
> G. B. Shaw

And who shops? Who cooks? Who *pays*? Who cleans the loo? A lot of men believe the tooth fairy does overtime: tea-bags, milk and the catfood are miraculously self-renewing. Petty resentments can so easily build in the first few months if one partner gets lumbered with more of the housework than another, so it's an extremely important time to establish a fair rota. I know it doesn't exactly smack of romance but then at least these petty issues might not separate you further on down the road. (Grounds for divorce. Violence? Infidelity? 'Nope, he just never, ever once put his dirty clothes in the wash, he didn't even know where the machine was . . . or the kitchen.') Trade with each other: I'll do this if you do that. If you both work, you should both contribute.

Sometimes, though, she has a different view of tradition from him:

Her view of fair trading:
  I cook . . . he washes up.
  I do the shopping . . . he drives and unpacks it all.
  I wash . . . he irons.

His view of fair trading:
  She cooks . . . I eat.
  She irons . . . I wear.
  She fills the cupboard with food . . . I empty them for her.

Other strange behavioural patterns some men develop having found a partner are:
a) Butter fingers. After having lived alone and survived quite well for years, suddenly, he'll burn the dinner, cut his hand putting shelves up, leave smears of glass polish all over the mirror. Don't be fooled, it's often deliberate, the bigger the mess, the greater the guarantee he'll never be asked to do it again. (And, OK, some women have been known to try this too, but they are getting better.)
b) Loss of memory. 'It's *tonight* your parents are coming over? Oh no! I'm still in a meeting' (ho, ho).

Sometimes she can find herself assuming the role of nag and never quite knowing how it happened:

She: 'Darling, would you mind putting out the rubbish?'
He: 'Don't I always?'
She: 'Well, no, actually, I usually do.'
He: 'Is this a complaint?'
She: 'No, a request. I've done everything else tonight, shopped, cooked . . .'
He: 'I didn't realize we were keeping scores! How long have you been holding this one in?'
She: 'I only asked if you'd put the rubbish out . . .'
He: 'I heard you the first time, don't nag.'

Sometimes you can't win. When men wonder what women's private fantasies are they might imagine exotic dreams about balmy nights of seduction and romance in the tropics, whispers of delights to come, stolen kisses and gasps of pleasure at the size of his magnificent manhood (well, it is *him* doing the fantasizing!). But in reality I believe her secret dreams go more like this:

She: 'Darling, would you mind putting the rubbish out?'
He: 'Sure and I'll do it right away, you know what I'm like for forgetting once I've settled down for the night. Would you like a glass of champagne while I start the dinner? I picked up a bottle of your favourite on the way home.'
She: 'My prince . . .'

TIPS FOR THE EARLY DAYS:

1) If you both work and you can afford it, get a cleaning lady.
2) Divide the chores equally and fairly, not so one gets all the 'nice chores' (buying the flowers) and the other gets all the rotten ones (hoovering, ironing).
3) If you can, buy two tvs or video recorders, so neither of you has to feel you have to give in to the other.
4) If, for example, he isn't comfortable with some of her friends and she's certainly not going to give them up, when you see them, go out in a crowd. Or if it's your turn to have them round for dinner and you can't say he's working late again because you've used that excuse fifty-four times, invite them on a night when a few people he does like are coming as well.

5) Don't make compromises so that neither of you is happy just for the sake of not upsetting your partner. Otherwise you'll end up with black and chrome furniture and pink frilly foo-foo curtains and cushions because neither of you would give in. Try letting him have full reign in the bathroom, she can do the hall and come to a compromise that's agreeable in the other rooms. These things *can* be sorted out if you're honest enough.

6) Give each other time, respect and space to express preferences so that one person doesn't take over making all the decisions.

7) Ideally, if you can afford it, buy a pad like Scarlett and Rhett's in *Gone with the Wind*, live in separate wings with a room somewhere in the middle of the house where you can meet if you feel like a bit of hot Southern passion or a take-away pizza.

3

PASSIONKILLERS

> *'Some are born with cold feet, some acquire cold feet and others have cold feet thrust upon them.'*
>
> Evan Esar

Let's assume you make it past the first minor hiccups and satisfactory compromises have been made. The fridge is full of mutually acceptable food and the organic alfalfa sprouts are comfortably tucked up next to his sliced white bread. The bathroom rota's working nicely and one morning he listens to the radio, the next morning she's allowed quiet. You've worked out your compromises and agreed to differ here and there. You look forward to settling down to life together, cosy and companionable. That's when you notice:

He: talks with his mouth full so you can see exactly what stage of mastication the salmon and broccoli's at; is never still and drums all the surfaces with his fingers; continually bites his nails; farts like a trooper; leaves his clothes exactly where he takes them off and prefers mindless tv to going out to mindless discos.

She: leaves her make-up all over the bathroom; wears her socks in bed; always interrupts when he's speaking; snores

and grinds her teeth; has a family who makes the Addams family look like the Waltons.

All those qualities that first endeared you to each other start to irritate:

Before: 'I love Chris because he has a wonderful child-like vision of life.'
After: 'Irresponsible bastard. I wish he'd grow up.'

Before: 'Charlotte's a breath of fresh air, at last a truly independent woman!'
After: 'Never at home when I want her, the cold, unfeeling, cow.'

Before: 'She's so vivacious, such a fabulous husky, deep voice.'
After: 'She never shuts up, that *dreadful* loud voice, I need a megaphone to be heard.'

Before: 'What I adore about Reggie is that he's *so* sensible and responsible.'
After: 'This man is driving me *mad* with boredom, why can't he *ever* do something spontaneously!'

Before: 'For once I feel loved, this girl is *so* affectionate and cuddly.'
After: 'I'm suffocating, she's so *clingy*, yerghh!'

Before: 'We just can't keep our hands off each other. At last a partner whose sex-drive matches mine!'
After: 'It makes my flesh creep just to look at her.'

Before: 'I'm in love, he's *too, too wonderful.*'
After: 'I'd rather chew my own liver than speak to that ass-wipe again.'

Irritating things that
you start to notice :

Ain't love grand? Ain't humans fickle? But what is it that happens to change our hearts and minds so radically?

1) Over-familiarity/boredom: the pleasure of each other's company can wane if couples weave a cocoon around themselves and shut the world out. Although this is tempting to do in the beginning it can be destructive in the long run. Old friends get ignored, independent interests abandoned and, in the end, as there's no new input or stimulation, people get bored. A bit of distance can help you see more clearly what attracted you in the first place.

2) Taking each other for granted: this has to be the most common complaint. 'The ratfink doesn't appreciate what I do for him, he doesn't even notice,' 'He never comments on how I look any more, I may as well not bother,' or 'I always buy her flowers and little gifts but never get any thanks for it.'

3) Lack of communication: if small resentments aren't expressed, they build up into big ones and a small incident can trigger a whole shopping list of grievances leaving the partner bewildered and defensive. Beware of the loaded silence when you ask your partner 'how are you?' and the reply is a tight 'fine', or you ask 'what's the matter?' and you're told curtly 'nothing'. Pursue these non-answers and find out what's behind them. It's always healthier to clear the air when it's appropriate and relevant than to store it up for years.

He: 'Darling, I'm home. What's for supper, sure smells good.'
She: '*Just* as I expected. You come in here, expecting your bloody tea, on time. Like every other day. Well, I'd had enough. Sod you. You never talk to me any

more, you mope about like a dead dog's dinner. You never remember my birthday or my mother's and last Christmas your present to me was the height of bad taste. In fact, I've hated everything you've ever bought me. And you can't kiss, it's like kissing a wet fish. And . . . that time we went to France eight years ago on holiday, don't think I've forgotten the way you looked at that tart in the restaurant. And you never help me with my luggage . . .'

'*She looks like Lady Chatterly above the waist and the gamekeeper below.*'
Cyril Connolly on Vita Sackville-West

4) Letting go of your appearance: 'not making an effort' is a big mistake. Don't forget there's a world out there of attractive offers, bargains and sales. If you've deteriorated from a spunky-looking show-stopper to a slob who lounges about in a misshapen dressing-gown, one day you may find yourself being ditched for this week's special offer. Part of the fun for both men and women is being proud of your partner. You don't want to be in a position where you want to say 'look what I managed to attract', and out staggers a Michelin man in flares or a hippie kaftan because that's all that'll fit. If yours won't take you out any more, maybe it's because they don't want to be seen with you and it's time to go to the gym.

5) Laziness: relationships do have to be worked at.

6) Selfishness: not pulling your weight is not only not fair but a recipe for separation.

7) Unrealistic expectations: before getting together it's a good idea to understand clearly what your partner's expectations are and if they match yours. If he wants a nymphette slave who's only entitled to her own opinion as long as it's the same as his, and she wants the male equivalent, things just might get difficult. And after being together a while, check the expectations haven't turned into 'ought to' and 'should'. You 'ought' to do this for me, I'm your partner, you 'should' be home when I say, it's how things 'ought' to be. According to whom? Her or him? And do you still agree?

8) Growing in different directions: when you first met you both voted liberal, were C of E, vegetarian and loved the countryside. Now he's taken up fox-hunting, converted to Catholicism, is running for the Tory party and has rented a penthouse overlooking Hyde Park. Whereas she joined the socialists, discovered Krishna

Murti, campaigns against cruel sports and discovered she likes a 'bit of rough' from the local builder on Tuesdays. (As does her husband . . . on Thursdays.)

9) Hard times always put a strain on a love affair. Poverty, unemployment or job insecurity can be demoralizing. If the funds are low:

(a) Make sure you still get out and have 'fun' times. Even if you can't afford your favourite restaurant any more, have friends round instead, and ask everyone to bring a dish. Or pack a picnic, get out somewhere cheap but different. Don't stay in moping, feeling you're a failure and can never be happy again. Go and watch people from a street café, there's no better show than the human race going about its business, it's free and in 3-D. Be inventive, discover the inexpensive side to your home town.

Try and understand what
Your partner is saying :

*glarrsk oom vöglenu
stom ob mogstd lognärr..*

ICELANDIC PHRASE BOOK

b) Learn to receive: if one partner's down on their luck, let the other one help. Sometimes it's difficult as it's easier to be the 'generous' one than the one who has to eat humble pie and let go of the control and independence that having extra cash gives.

c) Be positive about what you're going through. 'It's all part of life's rich tapestry.' (Or life's poverty-stricken tapestry.)

10) Try to understand what your partner is saying: this is done by a much under-used method called listening. And don't tell your partner what they think or put words in their mouth. (At least that's what my husband just told me to write.) Some areas can be remedied, some are too far gone. But let's go on to the one area that can cause the most trouble of all . . .

29

4

RESCUING THE ROMANCE

> *'A man marries to have a home but also
> because he doesn't want to be bothered with
> sex and all that stuff.'*
> Somerset Maugham

Many people believe that a lack of sex can be the cause of relationship break-ups. Personally, I believe it's more likely to be a lack of wardrobe space, but that's my own hang-up. Not enough cupboard space can also be a problem if you and your partner like doing it in strange places and there's only room for one of you in the 'magic wardrobe' to play 'Aslan from Narnia reprimands the horny White Witch'.

Several factors are thought to be responsible for taking the urgency out of the urge or vice versa.

1) Vitamin/mineral deficiency
2) Familiarity
3) Worry
4) Boredom
5) Bad health
6) Lack of exercise
7) Pressure at work
8) The secretary at work

9) Having a baby and children, lack of sleep, hormonal upset and all the joys that go with parenthood
10) Alcohol
11) Getting old, fat and droopy
12) Or just droopy

How to resolve the dilemma? The first step to finding your way is admitting that you're lost, something most men find difficult on the most basic level.

She: 'Let's stop someone and ask for directions, we're obviously totally lost.'
He: 'Rubbish. We'll find our way. Don't give in so easily.'
She: 'But we've been going round in circles for hours.'
He: 'Yes, but isn't it fun being on an adventure?'
She: 'I haven't had so much fun in years. Come to think of it, I haven't had *any* fun in years!'

It's important to recognize what's happening and admit it. From love being blind to turning a blind eye, the language of love starts to be Braille and unless you speak and understand it, sometimes it's a good idea to open your eyes and see the signs.

THE TELL-TALE CLUES:

> 'It's been so long since I made love, I can't even remember who gets tied up any more.'
> Joan Rivers

1) When you say your partner is 'good in bed', you mean he lies still, doesn't snore, fart or jiggle.
2) When your idea of a good night in bed is with a book and a cup of cocoa.
3) When you can't remember the last time you did it.
4) When you can't remember what *it* is.
5) When you say 'A partner like mine is hard to find', what you mean is does anyone know where she is?
6) When you say your partner is careless about his appearance you don't mean that he's put on a bit of weight. You mean he hasn't shown up for a few months.
7) When you say your partner loves you terribly that's exactly what you mean!
8) When he says he's willing to die for you, you're even more willing to let him.
9) When you come home to find a cosy romantic dinner, you know you've gone next door by mistake.

But enough of the down side that doesn't go down any more either. Is there hope? Solutions? Light at the end of the tunnel of love?

In order to recapture some of the gold-dust that was there in the beginning, it's a good idea to go back to there and start again very slowly.

Kissing: Reintroduce kissing. Often couples who've been together for a while go from no. 1 to 40, cold to hot in ten minutes and nothing in between. Whatever happened to the long sensual snogging sessions and a bit of 'hands on any parts that stick up or out' game.

Look after your looks: Take care of your appearance. Try to revive those early days, those sessions in front of the mirror: 'Oh I can't wear that, that'll give the impression I'm sex mad and have gone to too much effort. And this is too casual, don't want to give the idea I don't care at all. This is too trashy. This bra's too faded, but the new silk knickers are good,' and three hours later, perfumed and groomed, a vision of loveliness appears. And that's just his story.

It's important to carry on making an effort and not just fling any old thing on. Particularly if she or he resents being called 'any old thing'.

Flattery: Remember to pay each other sincere compliments. In the beginning they came thick and fast. Statements like 'Of course I love you. I'm still with you aren't I?' or 'I told you I loved you, remember Christmas 1968?' don't count. Notice haircuts, new clothes, a curve of the ankle, texture of the skin. Everyone needs appreciation and to feel special. No one can ever be told often enough that they are loved, wanted or admired.

Be adventurous: Don't just stay in for yet another vibrant night in front of the telly, get out and do something different. Court each other. Book special outings and weekends away. Together. (It's no fun getting to the airport only to find that your partner has booked your flight to Paris . . . and his to Milan.)

Make time: Make quality time together, not 'Howza 'bout it, fluff bunny?' just as both of you collapse into bed exhausted from the day. Arrange time for you to take time.

Surprise your partner: Just when he/she thinks they know all about you and how you respond to or initiate sex, surprise them. Try something new, wear something different – though more in the line of sensuality than inviting him to bed, turning down the lights then going 'Surprise! Whaddya think of my new "arrow through the head" hat!?'

Make a bridge: Often if she's been wiping babies' bums all day and is covered in dribble and sticky finger stains, it can take a while for her to turn into her other role as Nefertiti the temptress, love goddess of East Finchley. And if he's just

Surprise your partner :

had a gruelling day at work and a horrendous journey home, it's difficult to feel enthusiastic about anything besides just getting home and locking the world outside out. Make a bridge (not with the furniture, I mean metaphorically). Give each other a relaxing, non-sexual massage, take a long, fragrant bath. Unwind. Farm the kids out sometimes for the night (arrange to swop with other parents who have young kids). Give each other time and space to get in the mood.

5

SEX

> 'The wife should not go to bed in any old nightdress but should choose something short, frilly and transparent, and the husband should abandon those ugly, striped pyjamas for, say, a cossack-necked pyjama top and brief, tight fitting shorts'
> (From *Sex Power Over Forty* by Gilbert Oakley)

The old cliché for a fading sex life is the black see-through nightdress. Apparently one of you (preferably the female, but whatever turns you on) has to put on the nightie, answer the door with a rose placed tantalizingly between the teeth, a twinkle in the eye and a glass of wine in the hand. Most people I spoke to said this would make them burst out laughing rather than turn them on, so I would add a cheque book to the list – sometimes bribery works where all else fails.

But it's true that making love to the same old partner can get a bit boring. You may very well adore chocolate cake, but a diet of it every day can get a bit monotonous and a piece of cheesecake or Austrian apple strudel for a change can seem madly attractive. So what do you do? These are the options:

1) Try to have your cakes and eat them and hope none of the neighbours saw you.
2) Accept boredom as the price you pay for companionship.
3) Update the requirements: sexually, people's moods, desires and needs are changing all the time. Just because she liked a certain position when you first met, doesn't mean she likes it that way every time. Again. And again. Update the menu, tempt the palate with interesting variations. Find out what each other wants from day to day. After all, we'd never serve up exactly the same food

every day. We ask each other, 'What do you fancy tonight?' and adapt, see what's in the cupboard, plan menus and take turns to cook. Sometimes we're not even hungry, except for a snack, sometimes what's required is a five-course blow out, sometimes a taste of the Orient. Apply all of this to your love requirements and you can't go wrong.

> *'My husband is German, every night I dress up as Poland and he invades me.'*
> Bette Midler

4) Fantasize. A good male friend of mine pointed out, very wisely, that the logical step on from fantasy for him would be to go out and get himself a mistress. First the thought, then the action. Makes sense. That's the risk you take if you fantasize. Other friends said they thought fantasizing would be an insult to their partner. But it really depends on what or who the fantasy is. Are you role-playing, where you can still be yourselves playing dramatic parts and so discover and enact hidden parts of yourself? Or is it pure fantasy, and you wish your partner was your best mate's wife because she's got a cracking set of bazongas and you've always wanted to stick her one. Quite a moral debate really! So rather than pursue it, here are a few suggestions for games to play:

Catherine the Great and Big Neddie
Vikings and virgins
Dr Camel and the Arabian slave
Doctors and nurses
Nympho and the virgin prince
Bruce and Anthea (for the older generation)

Rambo meets the living dead (apparently this is one of
the two fantasies played most nights nationwide, so
scrap that one, and the other, King of the Zombies
meets the Zombie Queen, which is not much fun
either)
Be gentle, I'm an alien
Slow, steamy, sweaty
Teach me all, Casanova
Big Bimbo and the bank clerk
Blindfold and hot
Guess what I'm using now, Your Majesty
and finally, if you're really fat and flabby, try most
people's favourite fantasy: close your eyes and
imagine you've got a threesome going.

Games and role-playing that don't work:

Yoo, hoo! I'm a teapot
Scrabble

I'm not knocking these games, it's just that neither will
you be if you play them.

It also helps to change the location and the time. Friday
night, every third week, in the bed, in the missionary
position can become routine to say the least. Be inventive:
try the stairs, up against the wall, in the garden, over the
fence, the kitchen table. In a lift, in a box at the theatre. In
the afternoon. In the lunch break, book a hotel and sneak
away and do it in the taxi on the way. Make it fun.
Don't:

a) act as though you're doing your partner a favour ('Oh,
all right, seeing as it's you').

b) act as though it all makes you sick ('Don't get that revolting thing out when I'm having my tea').

c) act as though you want to get it over with ('Can you get a move on, so I can get back to my book').

d) be totally unresponsive ('Zzzzzzzzzzzzzzzz').

e) be too bossy and domineering (unless you're playing 'Bossy Bertha gets her come-uppance').

Seriously, though, sex is often blamed for partnership breakdowns, but it is usually only the symptom of something wrong on a far more fundamental level. So instead of blaming the symptom, it is actually far more effective to go back to the root and take a look at what can be done there.

6

THE SECRET

> 'The art of love? It's knowing how to join the temperament of a vampire with the discretion of an anenome.'
>
> E. M. Cioran

The root of a relationship is, in the end, how you get on as people. Is your communication clear? Or do weeks go by leaving much unspoken but not unknown? And who cares any more? You've learnt to step around each other. Is the relationship still alive or is it just a familiar state of mutually compromised existence that both of you are too lazy to change? ·

In a comprehensive survey of people who'd ever had, or were having a relationship they were asked what the secret to keeping love alive was. Here are some of the answers:

1) Lots of sex, sometimes with your partner.
2) Always do as *she* says.
3) It works best when one is slave to the other.
4) Bribery.
5) Realistic expectations. George Kaufman told Irving Berlin that the lyrics of his song 'Always' were un-realistic. Instead of 'I'll be loving you always', he suggested 'I'll be loving you Thursdays'.

The secret of keeping love alive:

It is easy if you follow these simple rules.

General

1. Have two bathrooms
2. Avoid each other most of the time.

Men

1. Have a big fat willie.
2. Have a big fat wallet

Women

1. Dress like a tart.
2. Stay out of the way until you're needed.

6) Compromise.
7) Space.

> '*Get married, but never to a man who is home all day.*'
>
> G. B. Shaw

8) Emotional blackmail.
9) Manipulation through guilt.
10) Independent interests.
11) Both being willing to work at it.

It's too easy, after having lived with someone for a while, to forget how your partner really is. So much can get left unsaid as we stumble through the daily routine of simple survival. Shopping, sleeping, laundry, working, looking after a family, weeks can go by without couples really talking to each other. Now most people don't imagine they are psychic, but are genuinely surprised to find that what they thought to be going on in their partner's head isn't the case at all.

He: 'Yes. Sara is a model wife. I trust her implicitly. She hasn't got it in her to stray. She loves our life together, it's all she ever wanted.'
Sara: 'I hate the low-down piece of scum, he's so smug. I'm off to Acapulco with the plumber.'

> '*Wives are people who feel they don't dance enough.*'
>
> Groucho Marx

Some of the women complained that they never felt acknowledged for their contribution, as though their time

and effort wasn't as important as their partners. And the men said the same about the women.

Some of the men complained that they felt misunderstood, and their partners put words into their mouths and told them what they were thinking. And the women said the same about the men.

She says she can do no more, she's put everything she's got into the relationship. And she has. He says he's given 100 per cent, there's nothing left to give. And he's right. But it's still not working.

Sometimes having a relationship is like pushing a car from the inside, puffing and straining till there's nothing left. It makes a hell of a difference to put the effort where it's effective. Get *out* of the car and push from behind and the results are immediate, you don't even have to make as much effort.

And that's the secret: put the effort where it's going to be effective. First you have to find out how. What does he actually want? What does she actually want? Are each

other's needs being met? Are these needs realistic? Do you listen to the hints?

Make your hints into statements that can't be mis-interpreted. Forget about being subtle if he/she didn't pick up on something after the first hint, make it clear what you want, tell him/her, make a poster, send them a telegraph: 'I want you home tonight 6 pm, for sex, bring a bottle and a friend.' (OK, possibly not a friend.) Acknowledge each other's presence. 'Oh, and how long have you lived here?' doesn't go down too well after a few years.

Support your partner in public: if one of a partnership is more articulate in arguments or more verbally aggressive in private, sometimes the other will wait until they have an audience at a party or dinner. They know their partner wants to be seen as the model mate and so won't retaliate, and then out come the poisoned barbs.

Hostess: 'Happy Birthday. And how old are you today, Jeremy?'
Jeremy: 'Thirty-four.'
The Partner: 'Talking about your IQ again, sweeeetie?'

10 FAVOURITE TIPS FOR A GOOD RELATIONSHIP:

1) Don't grumble, there's nothing like it for killing the passion. If you've got something to say, state your needs clearly and without blame. 'I need . . .' or 'I feel . . .' always works better than 'You never . . .'

   And if you can, baffle your partner into submission by being cheerful. Easier said than done but more effective in the long run.

   > *'It destroys one's nerves to be amiable every day to the same human being.'*
   > Benjamin Disraeli

2) Don't bury yourself away with your partner. Keep your friends, see them regularly.
3) Don't expect your partner to satisfy all aspects of your needs on every level and then hold them responsible when they can't. Ultimately, you are each responsible

for your own happiness. For example, if you massage your partner and do it well but when it comes to their turn they're hopeless at it, don't get frustrated and blame them. Find someone else who *can* do it, a friend you can trade skills with, or a professional and have some treatments on the house budget. Or if neither of you can do DIY or put the shelves up, instead of feeling inadequate and accusing each other of being a dead loss, concentrate on what you can do and contribute and get someone who can do the job properly in to do what you can't.

Always consider alternative methods of getting what you need. It's much more productive to look at what

the required end result is and then work out your options for achieving it, rather than blaming your partner for not achieving it. This is not a good idea to apply when it comes to sex however.

He [thinks]: She's not in the mood. Now, according to the book, I shouldn't waste time in futile reactions. What are the options open to me? The solution obviously is *get a professional.* Where's that card I found in the telephone kiosk? My wife's going to be really pleased I've grasped the concept of non-reactive-negative reconditioning. Saucy Sara does home visits for naughty sailors TEL. 96845 . . .

4) Find ways to let off steam. Sometimes a bad mood may

be nothing to do with your partner but they are the ones who get it if you don't release it somewhere else. Try:

a) buying a load of old plates from a reject shop. Next time you're in a situation where it's inappropriate to get angry (at work or stuck on the underground) wait till you get home. Get your plates out, assume the stance of a Sumo wrestler and with a loud warrior war cry slam the plates at the floor or at the wall. You'll feel instantly better and when it comes to the time your partner comes through the door irate from their hard day and journey home, you'll be smiling sweetly as you hand them *their* plates. A rather expensive and messy solution but better to take out frustration on a wall than on your loved ones, and it's cheaper than therapy or the divorce courts.

b) Try the Gestalt technique. Pick a couple of cushions, project on to them the personality or reason for your anger and punch, scream, rant, rave and kick away to your heart's content. An inexpensive method of getting your anger out and no one's hurt or affected (except the neighbours who think you're either barmy or have a very passionate sex life).

c) While driving in your car, wait until you're on a patch of road with trees on either side and no people about, then let rip. *Scream*. Let it all out. Tell your parents what you've always wanted to, insult your boss with words even you didn't know you knew. This really works wonders and gives a wonderful rush of energy. (If you ever see a car coming towards you with a vision of Edvard Munch's *The*

> *Scream* at the wheel, you'll know it's someone who's read this book and is giving it a try.)

5) Give each other acknowledgement for what each of you contributes. Don't only mention what isn't done or what's missing.

6) Respect your partner as an individual and don't just see them as another appendage to your life. Don't always say 'This is *my* choice of car, *my* choice of house and district, *my* choice of partner . . .'

7) Make time to talk. And listen.

8) Treat each other to surprises occasionally.

9) Make an effort to go out of your way to let your partner know you think they're special. If his favourite ice-cream is Häagen-Dazs, don't get him whatever's local and cheaper. He'll think that's how you view him and you can't be bothered. Get what he likes, maybe not as often as he'd like but you'll get more thanks for making an effort. If her favourite flowers are lilies, but buying them means going out of your way, go and get the lilies. You'll only have to do it once for her to remember you care enough to go out of your way, and she's worth that to you.

10) Give each other space. Dorothy Parker once said, 'Love is like quicksilver in the hand. Leave the fingers open and it stays. Clutch it and it darts away.'

But if none of this works perhaps it's time to seek professional guidance and see what they have to say . . .

7

WHAT THE EXPERTS SAY

> 'Marriage is the only war where one sleeps
> with the enemy.'
>
> Mexican proverb

According to the 'experts' all relationships are doomed. The stronger the attraction and sense of 'where do I know you from?' at the beginning, the bigger the problems are going to be later. The sexperts wouldn't put it quite like that, but that's what much of their advice amounts to!

The reason attraction guarantees nights of headbanging frustration (not the banging you had in mind) is that basically we are all looking for a partner with whom we can replay unresolved anxieties from our childhood. And so we remarry someone like our parents. Just when you thought you'd left home you find yourself back in it.

All those years of purple punk hair, no knickers and devil-may-care nights count for nothing, because you've become your mother — be it martyr, nag or know-it-all. And the wanton rogue with the wild spirit and tight jeans has just turned into your comfy old dad, and he's traded his Harley Davidson in for a Volvo. Sounds like doom to me, *and* there's no escape because apparently it's all unconscious anyway and we don't even realize we're doing it. Oh, horrible, horrible! Betrayed by our own unconscious!

The 'experts', however, would argue that it's not betrayal, it's behaviour designed to create a situation where it's possible to heal old wounds and rise above past painful experiences. How this works by endlessly repeating familiar patterns of destructive behaviour learnt in your early years beats me. But that's the theory. You have several choices:

1) You and your partner go to therapy for most of your remaining years and unlearn the bad attitudes.
2) You row a lot, feel like you're wading endlessly through a pan of cold porridge, stuck in the same old arguments time after time.
3) You get divorced, remarry and repeat the process with a younger version.
4) You lie, cheat, have affairs, drink, take drugs, overwork and generally avoid the situation as much as possible.

But since that's probably something you learnt to do from one of your parents this option isn't exactly an escape either.

5) Avoid that person in a crowd you feel attracted to, that person you feel you've always known. Run for it and go home with the doublebagger sitting in the corner. (A doublebagger is someone you find so sexually unappealing that not only do you wear a paper bag on your head, they also wear one on theirs, in case one of the bags tears and you catch sight of each other.) Well, it's one way to avoid pain, growth and transformation on any level and have a trouble-free relationship.

Remember there are many levels when dealing with the unconscious, the greater the attraction, the greater the challenge, and the more lessons you're going to learn with that person. If you see it through, you will emerge an older and wiser soul – evident by your benign nature and white hair.

By the same rule, the greater the abhorrence the less the challenge, you will remain carefree, unenlightened, un-evolved but will have fabulous skin and no grey hairs.

In the light of all of this if anyone says *any* of the following, don't say you weren't warned:

The Conscious Mind: I feel a sense of timelessness when I'm with you. Cor, I fancy you.
The Unconscious Mind: Mummy!!!

The Conscious Mind: Haven't we met before somewhere? Let me get my hands on you, you big sweaty hunk.
The Unconscious Mind: Yep, you're the one for me, you've the potential to turn out to be one moody son-of-a-bitch, just like my old man.

The Conscious Mind: I feel I've always known you, yes, yes, I've scored!!

The Unconscious Mind: Yoh! Are *we* in for a miserable marriage, just the situation I need to heal all my childhood hurts and discover that actually I'm OK. And when I do, I dump you . . . which is perfectly in synch with your abandonment pattern set up when your parents left you on a doorstep! Couldn't be better.

Conscious Mind: Ugly sucker, I'm not going home with you tonight even if you pay me.

The Unconscious Mind: No potential conflict here, no evolution of the species, no drama, therefore no entertainment for the big boss upstairs in the sky.

The other theory popular with the experts is that we are all attracted to someone who manifests the hidden, undeveloped or dark side of our nature. Hence when they behave in a manner we find strange or offensive, it is actually a reflection of ourselves we are objecting to and given the chance, permission or encouragement we'd behave the same way. The only solution is to identify these hidden selves and so understand why we overreact to them in our partner. It is really because we recognize some aspect of ourself that we don't want to admit to, that we come into conflict. Instead of projecting the dark side on to our partner and letting them play it all out and annoy us, we should play it out ourselves.

This can get mighty confusing, though, because it can be used as an excuse for every bit of trouble we ever get into.

She: 'You louse, I hate you. You're a drunk, a womanizer and a slob.'

He: 'I knew it. It's all a reflection of yourself and secretly you're a lazy, alcoholic lesbian.'

She: 'Oh God! According to the "experts" you're right. But if I think that *you're* right then that must mean, according to the reflection theory, that *I'm* right after all. I'm so confused I think I'll shoot myself, or should I shoot *you* or the reflection of you which is *me*? Help!!?'

It's all a set-up as far as I'm concerned, we've been programmed to perversely enjoy a challenge, there are no real easy options. But there are a few ways to make life easier . . .

8

WHAT THE REALISTS SAY

> 'Marriage is the alliance of two people, one who never remembers birthdays and the other who never forgets them.'
>
> Ogden Nash

There are several schools of thought on how best to survive living with someone of the opposite sex.

a) be honest, open and considerate
b) lie, cheat and manipulate

It is b) that we are going to look at in this chapter (see previous chapters for the other approach).

THE ANCIENT ART OF MAKING EXCUSES

If you're the kind of person who's persistently unreliable and abysmally forgetful and it's threatening your relationship, the following guide is for you.

The rules:

1) Always remember what excuse you gave, otherwise
   He: 'I'm so sorry I couldn't make your brother's wedding. I was in Alabama for a conference.'
   A year later:
   The brother: 'How was your trip to Alabama?'
   He: 'Alabama? I've never even been to the States, let alone . . . whoops . . .'
2) If you say you are staying in a particular hotel or place, first check that it exists, otherwise,
   She: 'Stayed at the Dog and Sausage Arms, Potholeingham, did you? You slimy nappy bucket. Wasn't it uncomfortable sleeping in a cinema seat? It changed hands in 1976!!' (whack)
3) Keep handy props in the car boot:
   a) Stick-on spots. 'Sorry I'm late, I came out in this rash and just had to have it checked in case it's contagious.'
   b) A permanently flat tyre. 'Sorry I'm three hours late. Damn flat tyre!'
   c) A clamp. 'Damn clampers, can't park anywhere these days, soooo sorry.'
   d) An inflatable sick grandma. 'Sorry, can't stay, got to get Gran seen to.'
   e) A rubber dead cat. 'Darn thing just ran out in front of the car, guess I'm gonna have to search the area till I find poor Tiddles' owner, sorry I can't stay.'
   f) A broken watch. 'Hell, is *that* the time? My watch must be wrong! Nope, worse, darn thing's stopped!'
   g) A broken leg cast. '*So* sorry! Bit of an accident!'
   h) Assorted neutral presents (champagne, chocolates, scent). 'It's your birthday?!!! . . . Of course, I'll just go and get your present, I left it in the car.'
   i) Pale stage make-up: 'Ooooh! I don't feel very well. I might have to leave this *fabulous* party early.'

4) Excuses for the phone:
   a) 'Sorry I haven't called. My address book was stolen.'
   b) 'I've been trying to get through for hours. I've called the GPO, they said there was a fault on the line.'
   c) 'Hi, thanks for calling, at last. Yes, I did call you but your answering machine wasn't on. What! It was? Let me check the number, 234 6789? Oh no, I had 234 6788, sooooo sorry.'
   d) 'I left loads of messages on your tape. What, you didn't get them? Actually the message did sound a bit odd, perhaps there's something wrong with it. I'd have it checked if I was you.'
   e) 'I called – you must have been out. Oh, you've been in all the time? I must have called when you were on the loo.'

   And for cutting calls short, have a door bell ringer close to the phone, 'Sorreee, got to go, that's my taxi.'

As the art of believable excuse-making is in keeping them varied, here's a random selection to work your way through: the Northern line; sickness; children; friend in need; traffic; demonstrators marching; roads blocked off; astrological omens; cash point that didn't work; phone boxes that have been vandalized; car broke down; animal in need of the vet; car broken into; jury service.

Advanced Excuses:

If you keep getting lumbered with your partner's friends or family, try answering your front door with your coat on. Depending on who it is: 'Hi! I just got in, come in.' Or 'Hi, just on my way out, I'll walk you back to your car.'

Don't just settle for a brief excuse and apology, when you can fabricate a really long complicated story. The more

outrageous, the better: 'You just won't believe what happened to me today. There I was on my way here, train's on time for once, when a tree goes and falls across the line. Of course, British Rail said it was the wrong kind of tree and couldn't shift it for a week. So we all had to get out and this poor pregnant lady slipped on the bank and fell. I ran to the nearest phone box to call 999 for her – not my day, got bloody locked in it, didn't I? One of those old rusty jobs with big, heavy doors. Was there for hours before anyone'd help me out, passers-by thought I was some sort of lunatic banging on the glass and then . . .'

The listener (thinks): 'Zzzzzzzzzz. He couldn't possibly have made this up, it must be true.'

And, of course, there's the quick thinking required when caught up to no good:

Two naked lovers hear the husband coming up the stairs:

She: 'Quick, hide in the bathroom.' (He scarpers off.)
The husband goes straight to the bathroom and finds a naked man in there clapping the air intermittently with his hands.
Lover-boy: 'Morning, Mr Parsons, I'm from Insect Repellers, Little Wopping. Your wife called me in about the dreadful moth invasion you've had lately (clap). Oops, there goes another of the little bastards. (Looks down at his body.) 'Oh, *no!* They've eaten *all* my clothing!!!'

HOW TO GET YOUR OWN WAY

> *'Diplomacy is the art of letting someone else have your way.'*
> Daniele Vare

a) A good technique for getting a reluctant partner to do things your way is to make them think it was their idea in the first place. Slowly introduce the idea, no pressure, no 'I have to have a decision on this *now.*' . . . Leave it, discuss it again a week later. Let it slip that your suggestion is definitely the one agreed with by anyone in the know and anyone not agreeing would be thought of as moronic. Let the idea grow, then a week later ask if he/she ever thought of enacting that fabulous idea they had. By this time, the idea has become theirs and they insist on it being put into action immediately.

She: 'Darling, how about Kenya for the next holiday?'

He: 'No way, never, ever. Anyway, I don't want to talk about it now, "Twin Peaks" is starting on the telly.'

One week later:

She: 'I see David Lynch is shooting "Twin Peaks", part 2 in Kenya next year. Apparently he was totally blown out by the views.'

He: 'Really?'

She: 'Look, there's some photos in *Harpers* this month.'

A week later:

She: 'I been thinking about your Kenya idea, are you still keen to go?'

He: 'Picked up the tickets yesterday.'

Apparently, this always works better on the male of the species as most females are wise to the technique, having been trained from an early age by their mother.

One man I spoke to said, 'Men are not so stupid or naive as to fall for a stunt like that. At least that's what my girlfriend told me to say.'

b) And there's the no nookie if I don't get what I want technique (but this only works in the early days).

He: (at the moment of great passion, pant, pant) 'Oh, now, now, I'm comi . . .'

She: (rolling over) 'No, you're not, not unless you give in and let me have my way.'

He: 'Yes, yes, whatever, whenever . . . Just don't stop!'

A bit further down the road, this method may have to be revised and changed.

He: 'You can have whatever you want as long as we don't have to do it.'

She: 'Fine, just sign this cheque and I'll make us a nice cup of Horlicks.'

c) If a partner is behaving badly and doesn't respond to confrontation, mirror their behaviour. If he stays out late one night, you stay out later the next. If she fails to let you know she'll be late on a night you are cooking, when she cooks, you do the same. If he farts, go for a curry and floor him with a silent but deadly. If you can't beat 'em, join 'em.

But what's sauce for the goose is sauce for the gander and can lead to complications and the next chapter.

9

INFIDELITY

> '*Husbands are like fires, they go out if unattended*'
>
> (Zsa Zsa Gabor)

Often when one of two partners starts having an affair it's because there's something missing in the relationship. Usually what's missing is one of the partners, twice or three times a week.

If this is OK with you both, no worries. If it's not OK and you think your mate is keeping it up, with somebody else, then you have several options:

1) Shoot the bastard.
2) If it's the man who's strayed, consult your copy of *101 uses for a dead husband*. After you've shot him, have him stuffed with a stiffee on and put him in the hall as a hat stand, coat rack or for hoopla when you have guests.
3) Turn a blind eye.
4) Try and get to the root of the cause of the straying and see if it can be remedied.
5) Split up.
6) Sauce for the goose, sauce for the gander, anything you can do, I can do better.

'*Few things in life are more embarrassing than the necessity of having to inform an old friend that you've just become engaged to his fiancée.*'

W. C. Fields

Messing around is always a risk and usually ends in tears before bedtime for everyone involved at some stage. Sometimes it brings a couple back together as they realize what they stand to lose and what they mean to each other. But not always. In fact, rarely.

Many people say once the trust has gone, it can never be reestablished. In which case, if you've been naughty and it *really* meant nothing, it was just a one-night stand and you regretted it straight after and don't intend to do it again, sincerely and double-dead honestly, then keep your mouth shut and don't load it all on your partner. Just because you want to clear your conscience and you feel so guilty, why ruin their life as well.

If it's been going on a while and your mate suspects, don't tell them they're crazy and ought to get help for imagining such ridiculous things. It can be really damaging to cause someone to doubt their own intuition. And even more insulting to let them find out from some 'well-meaning' friend. Perhaps it's time to open it up, think about what you want and have the courage to live by that. (Easier said than done.)

If you keep doing it, regret it, get away with it, but can't stop yourself, apparently bromide does the trick. Or, on second thoughts, why not try cyanide.

But if your relationship is basically good but a little dry round the edges and you've only thought about straying, then, stop now and try out the survivor's guide in the last chapter.

10

AND FINALLY

> 'For even as love crowns you, so shall he crucify you. As he is for your growth, so is he for your pruning.'
>
> Kahlil Gibran

In the end, it has to be said that every relationship has its ups and downs and some you win, some you lose. But unless being with someone makes you more unhappy than happy over a prolonged period of time, it's always worth working at. Why not give the following exercises a try. They may help, they may not. At least they'll give you a few laughs and you may discover a thing or two about each other. Like you're totally incompatible and it's a miracle you lasted so long!

EXERCISES TO HELP KEEP IT UP

> *'Sex is work.'*
> Andy Warhol

First of all agree to put time aside every week to go through the programme. Sit down with your diaries and book an appointment with each other for a time you can be undisturbed. Try and make it a time when neither of you is going to be exhausted. Even if it means booking a babysitter to allow you to go as far as the back room and shut the door. We take time for friends, business colleagues and family but leave no time for each other, hoping things will just sort themselves out given time. Sometimes they do, but other times there comes a point where couples haven't been out alone for years. And the prospect can be terrifying.

EXERCISE ONE (ONE HOUR)

Laughing together is as important as sex, it can certainly be as enjoyable and you really hit the jackpot if you can do them both together. Unlike the woman who was with a lover who'd decided to impress her with an imaginative method of getting her kit off. He stealthily moved down her body, deadly serious, removing her clothing with his teeth, when, suddenly, eyes intent on his purpose and tugging on a reluctant zip, he fell over backwards, off the bed on to the floor, dislodging his dentures! What had started out as a way of taking her clothes off with his molars ended up with a set of pearls he hadn't accounted for.

She roared with laughter but he'd had his pride hurt and had to go straight home to nurse it, missing out on a night that could have simply continued on the floor.

This exercise is really simple.

1) Buy the local paper or magazine that lets you know what's on at the movies, theatre and local cabarets around town.
2) Spend a leisurely half hour looking through what's on offer.
3) Pick something you'd like to see that is agreeable to both of you, and go out and have a good laugh together.

EXERCISE TWO (ONE HOUR)

Questionnaire time. Yippee. Put aside any prejudices about forms and bureaucracy and get your pen out. No! . . . Your *pen!*

Get out some paper. Two sheets each. You're going to find out how you'd score on the 'How well do you know your partner?' TV game?

1) Throw a coin to see who reads the questions out.
2) Go through the questions in the questionnaire below. On the first sheet, write down what you *think* your partner's answers would be. Then on the second sheet of paper write down your own answer.
3) When you've finished, give your partner the first sheet (the answers you think they'd put) and keep the second sheet yourself. So each of you should now have a sheet of your own answers and the answers you think your partner thinks you would have given.
4) Whoever didn't read the first time now reads the questions again.
5) You each read out the answers in front of you.
6) You get one point for every answer that matches and that you got right.
7) Add up the scores at the end. The winner gets a cup of tea in bed in the morning and the loser has to sleep in the wet patch next time you have mad, rampant sex (which if you're following this guide will be very soon).

The check-list questionnaire:

1) What's their/your favourite colour?
2) What's their/your favourite flower?
3) What's their/your favourite restaurant?
4) What's their/your favourite food?
5) Where would they/you like to go on holiday next?
6) Would they/you like to go on holiday a) alone with their/your partner? or b) with a crowd of friends.
7) What annoys them/you?
8) What makes them/you happy?
9) What could make them/you happier?
10) How do they/you like to be kissed?
11) Where do they/you like to be kissed?
12) What can turn them/you off sexually?
13) What turns them/you on sexually?
14) What are the three most important qualities of their/ your perfect relationship? (e.g.: good sex, good

communication, shared sense of humour, values, independence, respect etc).

15) Which of their/your needs go unmet in your relationship?

16) What could they/you do to improve your relationship?

17) What would they/you like to change about your relationship?

EXERCISE THREE (ONE HOUR)

Crack open a bottle of wine for this if you both drink, otherwise get out the Vimto and crisps.

The pressure to succeed is present in just about every dimension of our lives. To succeed at work, to succeed at home. The pressure to 'pick up' on hints can be mindbendingly exhausting. Was he trying to tell me something then? Did I do it right? And then the peer group joins in as well.

'Yoh, Nigel, what you doing for the old lady's birthday? Something special? Last month's at the Brenmans' was a do to remember, eh?' And the next thing you know, you're competing with the Brenmans and who cares what the birthday girl wants, she's gonna get what looks good.

1) On a sheet of paper write down your idea of a perfect, romantic night with your partner. (It can be in or out, the evening that is, not a part of his anatomy, although that can be part of the menu as well, if you choose). Keep your plan within the realms of possibility but put in lots of detail. For example:

   a) Time to get ready and have a long soak in a scented bath before leaving.

   b) A taxi to pick us up for a change, so we don't have to argue about who can drink.

And so on (20 minutes).

2) Do the same for your idea of a perfect weekend. Again lots of detail (20 minutes).

3) Do the same for how you see your perfect birthday (20 minutes). Update this information year by year as it may change.

4) Swap papers and discuss any areas that are not clear. (Take as long as you like.)

Polish off the wine, get out your diaries and book the times that are convenient for both of you. Organize each other's dates and weekends for each other at some time in

the next three months. (And obviously the birthday treats on the birthday.)

Too much time is wasted hoping a partner will pick up on subliminal messages about what we want. Why not just tell them clearly! It's a wonderfully romantic notion that 'the One' will be able just to *know* exactly what to say, how to touch you, what to do or not. It only happens like that in old black and white movies.

People often give their partner the 'surprise' that they would like for themselves. For example, one woman said her husband arranged an elaborate birthday surprise party. Lots of people, entertainers, no expense spared. She could see he'd put a lot into it, so didn't dare say anything but she hated it and was hoping for a quiet romantic dinner on her own with him. He'd arranged the party *he* wanted, he'd never even found out what she'd have liked.

EXERCISE FOUR (TWO HOURS)

Sit down together. Get out a timer. The exercise is in five stages.

1) Writing (15 minutes for each list) = 30 mins.
2) Speaking (10 minutes each) = 20 mins.
3) Each reads out their first list while the other listens (10 minutes each) = 20 mins.
4) Discussing the first lists (30 mins).
5) Each reads out their second list while the other listens (10 minutes each) = 20 mins.

Stage 1) Take two sheets of paper and on one write all the

things you like about each other. The list can be as long as you like, in fact, the longer the better. On sheet two, write all the things that you don't like that are *rectifiable*. For example:

OK: 'I don't like the fact you never remember our anniversary.'

NOT OK: 'I don't fancy you now that you've lost all your hair and are as bald as a coot.'

Winston Churchill would have thought twice about his famous reply to Bessy Braddock if he'd read this guide. When she told him he was drunk he replied, 'And you, madam, are ugly, but I shall be sober in the morning.'

You have fifteen minutes to do each list, so write what comes straight into your mind. (That is unless you can't think of anything you like or don't like about your partner, in which case I suggest you start by writing, 'I don't like my partner because I can't remember much about them.')

Stage 2) Start the second part by saying, in turn, why you chose to be with each other. (It doesn't matter that some of this will be repeated on your 'Like' list.) The idea is to start by acknowledging what's good about your relationship. It's a well known fact if you 'sandwich' the bad news between some good it is much more palatable and you don't go smack into someone's defences. (You have ten minutes each on this.)

Stage 3) Agree not to comment as each reads their list, just listen. This can be difficult as there is always the temptation to butt in and say 'Wrong as usual, you rotten scab on a camel's bum.'

Stage 4) Each in turn, listen to what your partner has written and, when the first lists are finished, discuss your reactions and any you think are unreasonable. Give each other time to talk and consider the points they've raised even though you might not agree. Talk about any points

that you feel are reasonable and what you intend to do about them. (Allow yourselves 30 minutes for this part.) Stage 5) Now get out your 'Like' list, no matter if you are ready to murder each other by now read them out. Try not to spit. You'll find the atmosphere will mellow.

Keep to the time allotted or you may find you get stuck on some bits and run out of time before you complete the exercise. Or you may find that you are discussing one of you more than the other. The exercise and time is for both of you. Keep your partner's lists through the week and take time before the next exercise to re-read and consider what they said.

EXERCISE FIVE (FORTY MINUTES)

Give each other a non-sexual massage to re-introduce the pleasure of touch without any of the pressure of having to perform, please or be pleased sexually. Again, this is an area where people hope their partner will pick up signals, thinking it'd be cold and unromantic to be too specific. But the pressure to 'get it right' can make you want to give up in the end. Why not take the simple route, tell each other what you want. Twenty minutes each. Take turns.

1) Throw a dice to see who does what first. One 'is done' and directs. The other does the massaging. If you're the one being done, give directions as to how you want to be touched and where: the feet rubbed gently in peach oil, for example.
2) On her go, this time she lies down and gives directions and he has to follow them, for example: the neck, firmly, with jasmine oil for scent and some romantic music in the background.

EXERCISE SIX (ONE HOUR AND TEN MINUTES)

1) Take a sheet of paper each and write down any of the needs that you feel are unmet. Don't just confine it to needs you expect your partner to meet, also look at:

    Career needs (job satisfaction, goals)
    Creative needs

Spiritual needs
Communication
Emotional
Physical (relaxation time, diet, exercise)
Sexual

Sometimes when living with someone, the neglect felt by one comes as a complete surprise to the other. Sometimes your partner cannot meet your need and yet is being blamed. Communication is all it takes to realize what's going on. (Take half an hour to do your list.)

2) Read out what you have written in turn without comment (ten minutes each).

3) Discuss in turn what you can do to help each other meet your needs. For example, perhaps one of her needs is for more affection, with this, he can make more effort. One of his needs may be a quiet place to work at home without disturbances. Together they can discuss alternatives rather than him blaming her every time he's disturbed from his work by the phone, visitors or kids (half an hour on each).

Take longer if you need to but ensure that it doesn't become lopsided and one assumes the role of 'in need' and the other that of 'I'm OK, it's you who needs attention'. We all need it.

EXERCISE SEVEN (ONE HOUR)

Follow my leader. A familiar complaint amongst couples is that one of them is always the one to initiate sex while the other always has to be persuaded. So a week of taking turns!

1) Spend 10–20 minutes with a sheet of paper each. Cut the paper into ten pieces. On each piece write down ten pleasurable things (non-sexual) that you would like your partner to do to you. For example: bake me some American fudge brownies; get me a video from the hire shop; flatter me non-stop, convincingly, for 10 minutes; give me a neck massage for 15 minutes.
2) Read them out to your partner and tear up any he/she feels they either couldn't do or wouldn't like to have done. Rewrite and discuss until you have twenty mutually agreed ideas.
3) Fold all the pieces up and put them in a hat.
4) Get out the coin or dice to see who goes first.
5) One week it's his turn to be leader, she's not allowed to ask for sex, no matter how lusty she's feeling.
6) The next week it's her turn.

Of course, there will be weeks when he's leader but she's not in the mood and vice versa. In which case, the one who's not in the mood has to pick a penance out of the 'kill-joy' hat-dip.

Finally, you want to know what love really is:
Love is . . . waiting until a bad haircut has grown long enough to be reshaped before exclaiming, 'What the f**k have you done to your hair?'
And finally, finally:
Love is . . . not always having to have the last word.